HUGH MCMILLAN is a poet from Penpont in Dumfries and Galloway. He has written five full collections of poetry and has read at events and poetry festivals worldwide. His pamphlet *Postcards from the Hedge* was a winner of the Callum Macdonald Prize in 2009, a prize he won again for *Sheepenned* in 2017; as part of that prize, he became Michael Marks Poet in Residence for the Harvard Summer School in Napflio, Greece. He was also a winner of the Smith Doorstep Poetry Prize and the Cardiff International Poetry Competition. *Devorgilla's Bridge* was shortlisted for the Michael Marks Award and in 2015 was shortlisted for the Basil Bunting Poetry Award. In 2014 Hugh was awarded the first literature commission by the Wigtown Book Festival to create a work inspired by John Mactaggart's *The Scottish Gallovidian Encyclopaedia* (1824); *McMillan's Galloway* was published in limited edition in 2014 and in a revised edition from Luath in 2015.

MICHAEL ROBERTSON was brought up at Old Barr, Sanquhar. His father was a shepherd and there was never any doubt he would follow in his father's footsteps. He has now been herding in his own right now for over 20 years with the last 19 of them spent at Clonrae Farm at Tynron. In his own words, 'It's a great way of life and the only one I know.'

By the same author:

Tramontana, Dog and Bone, 1990
Horridge, Chapman, 1995
Aphrodite's Anorak, Peterloo Poets, 1996
Strange Bamboo, Shoestring, 2007
Postcards from the Hedge, Roncadora Press, 2009
Devorgilla's Bridge, Roncadora Press, 2010
Cairn, Roncadora Press, 2011
Thin Slice of Moon, Roncadora Press, 2012
All the Creatures in the Wood, Mariscat, 2014
McMillan's Galloway, privately printed, 2015
Not Actually being in Dumfries, Luath Press, 2015
McMillan's Galloway: A Creative Guide by an Unreliable Local,
Luath Press, 2017
Sheepenned, Roncadora Press, 2017
Heliopolis, Luath Press, 2018

The Conversation of Sheep

HUGH McMILLAN

with photographs by Michael Robertson

Luath Press Limited

EDINBURGH

www.luath.co.uk

To the forlorn landscape of Dumfries and Galloway
and all those who live, love, and graze on it

First published 2018
Reprinted 2018
Reprinted 2019
Reprinted 2021

ISBN: 978-1-912147-79-3

The paper used in this book is recyclable. It is made
from low chlorine pulps produced in a low energy, low emission
manner from renewable forests.

Printed and bound by Ashford Colour Press, Gosport

Typeset in 11 point Sabon by Main Point Books, Edinburgh

Contents

Acknowledgements 7

A Very Small Miracle 9
The Morning Moon 10
Sheep Feedback Forms 13
Confined 14
Choruses 16
Part of the Picture 19
Hame Grund 20
Argan 23
Looking for LaLa 24
The Conversation of Sheep 27
The Conversion of Sheep 28
Nocturne 31
Leader Sheep 32
The Dark Ages 35
Sheep on a Snow Ridge 36
The Ettrick Shepherd 39
Sheep Dog 40
James Hogg's Dog Blackie 43
Sheep Came Down at Christmas 46
Sheep Poets Workshop Prompts 48
Settlement 51
Cycle 52
Old Tracks 55

Sahil Island 56
The Golden Fleece 58
The Path between the Mountains of the Moon 61
Shooters 63
The Old Fort at Grennan 64
What Sheep Know 66
Quhit Yowes Ken 67
A Sheep and Duck Travel on the First Balloon Flight 69
The Shades of one Shade 70
Destiny 72
The View 75
Spring 76
The Adoration of the Shepherds 79
The Sound of Sheep Is Like the Sound of Poetry 80
Fighting Sheep 82
The Trouble with Science 85
The Inadequacy of Sheep Metaphors 87
Castle Sheep 89
Simple Truths 90
Wire 93
After the Sheep 94
Come Live with Me 96
December in Penpont 99
Sheep Ends 101
The Bird on the Sheep's Back 102
Circles 104
King of the Sheep 107

Acknowledgements

Some of the poems in this book appeared previously in the pamphlet *Sheepenned* (Roncadora Press) which won the Callum MacDonald Prize in 2016. 'Conversion of Sheep' appeared in *The Dark Horse*, *Heliopolis* (Luath, 2018) and in *Best Scottish Poems* (SPL, 2016). 'A Small Miracle' appeared in *Ten Poems about Sheep* Vol. 2 (Candlestick Press). Some of the other poems have appeared in *The Rialto*, *Gutter*, *The Antigonish Review* and *Compass Magazine*. The picture of Dolly the Sheep on page 86 is by Hugh McMillan.

A Very Small Miracle

A lamb was born near Dunnet Head,
tumbling in a yellow broth of legs
on the dark earth,
finding its feet just before
the brawling wind from the skerries did.
Nobody paid much heed.
The ewes were not easily impressed
by gyniatrics and two old women
talked on about tomatoes.
There wasn't even a farmer there
to count this a triumph for finance.
The dreaming lamb wobbled
on the lip of cool reality.
At thirty seconds old it had felt
the first rough edge of a tongue
and already knew that life
was not a bed of turnips,
at a minute
it was standing quite still
staring rudely at me,
as if it knew that being born
a sheep here
in these extremes of circumstance
was a very small miracle indeed.

The Morning Moon

I watch the hill with that moon
like a disc like an ice hole
and all the lustre
beyond it spilling out,
the sheep by the water
the hedgehogs in the wood
the kids in their beds
touched by the same light,
all suddenly brilliant creatures
of the moon.

It is like the pause between
thought and action,
a sacred space,
but they will rise and snuffle
and bleat and the world will recoil
trembling like out of a dream
though some may half remember
in a shadow of warmth,
or the brush of lips,
the print of the moon's passing.

Sheep Feedback Forms

'An artist has delivered a 45 minute lecture on the Highland Clearances to a flock of sheep to stimulate fresh debate on the historic events. Anthony Schrag's lecture in a field on a farm in Sutherland was filmed so it could be viewed by people living in and near the Strath of Kildonan.'

'Unlike other local artistic events eg the sheepdog trials there was no wine and canapés.'

'Sheep being lectured to by someone supported by creative Scotland was an irony that escaped him I think.'

'Was I the only sheep to feel patronised?'

'Poor seating. We felt herded together.'

'I came along expecting a more developed analysis to be frank.'

'Aren't there as many artists in Kildonan as sheep these days?'

'A good day out. Nice the rain kept off.'

'The most intellectual day I've had since the Library Vans were axed.'

Confined

Sun through an open door.
Outside, a staircase leads to nowhere
but sky and pines
spread like a hand over the mountain.

Inside is a shelf of books, a tumbler,
some tangerines, and worse,
a painting of a shepherd doomed
never to get sheep to the end of a potholed road.

It is a poor exchange for longevity
to be trapped between the desert and the sea,
the paint and the plaster,
the breath and its absence.

Choruses

Of all the layers of noise
inlaid like scrimshaw
on this ivory evening,
the piping birds
the soft prayers of trees,
the hiss of rain like breath,
the persistent crying
of lambs is the most piercing.
Their first tear filled night.

Part of the Picture

Winter is in the hills
grids of wall and white,
and nothing but sheep
spiked
against the wind,

and who best to know
pain, their children gone
year after year forever?
They share the loss
but bear it better.

In good days they turn
faces to the sun
then, knowing when
to disappear,
become part of the picture.

Hame Grund

Joseph Farquharson
was called frozen mutton
in society because of the number
of sheep that appeared
in his landscapes, paintings
invariably mired in winter
as he loved the north east coast,
snell an aye coovert wi snaw.

He counted these people his friends
though sometimes he wondered.
He painted what he saw
and he saw lots of sheep.
You wonder why
in the face of such skill
and power they sought
tae scrieve him in sic a coorse licht.

Behind the sheep,
sometimes instead of sheep,
he conjured such cadences
of ice and frost magically
twisted like torques
the sheen like old fire,
the complex twist like the grasp
livin an deein haes roon the thrapple.

I think his peers knew peasants
in the Auvergne at sunset
were best to draw:
at night you could toast draughtsmanship
in fine wines. They thought
Farquharson in his frozen hide
at the ridiculous rim of the world
hid bin driven reid mad by his cauf grund.

Argan

Goats climb the Argan tree
their small feet on the tiniest twigs.
They bend and sway, know the balance.
There are leaves on the Argan tree
still, though less trees:
it is the way of the world.
The topmost branches
put little goats among the stars
right there in the firmament
where constellations form,
where births begin of stars and goats
and trees. The beginning
and start of the dizzy end.

Looking for LaLa

I find LaLa pressed between the bath
and the wall. At some point between
the end of infancy and Taylor Swift's
issue of *Fearless* in January 2010,
she must have come down
the TellyTubby Island slide
in her shepherdess tunic
and, unnoticed in a storm of foam
and hormonal mist, dropped straight out of life.

I always liked her,
with her yellow beach ball and tutu,
and her suggestions of a dystopian world
where flowers are speaking tubes,
and people live in Eco bunkers
with intelligent hoovers:
like Switzerland,
except without the Nazis.

What now for her? She will sit between
the nail varnish and deodorants
and dream of lost sheep,
a tender archive, till sometime in a future
more strange than TV, more horrifying
than a corner full of spider webs even,
she will fall behind the dressing table
of an empty room.

The Conversation of Sheep

Where are the sheep of our imagination?
Ghostly in the dank moss of their fathers,
before the age of quadbikes,
before dykes even,

gazing at the sky or ocean
moving their jaws
as if a word might be there,
passing this on to the unborn,

sure in the conviction
that somewhere, maybe on a hill
like this with frost gleaming,
a sheep will begin the conversation.

The Conversion of Sheep

When St Fillan first came upon the sheep
they stood with their Sumerian heads
and stared him out,
for it is a fact that though sheep are mentioned
many times in the bible,
it is always in a bad way.
Follow me said St Fillan,
I have a new path and he pointed
into the hills, to where the sun was rising
setting the gorse to blaze.
They had seen many
paths and sunrises,
you might say they were
inured to them.
They had grass here,
green enough,
and every second Thursday
a book group,
due to discuss that night the third of
Naguib Mahfouz's *Cairo Trilogy*,
illustrating existentialism
in a non-Western context.
Nevertheless they saw
the fine pitch of madness
in the old man's eyes
and, reminding themselves
they were essentially
compliant herd animals,
followed.

Nocturne

This evening all
the greens have welled
into the sky like lilies.
The sheep are
stepping stones to heaven.
I imagine leaping
from each supple back
and each spring
lengthens and deepens
till from the last sheep
chewing uncertainly
on the last blade of grass
I bound like an arrow
fired from a bent bow
into the dark.

Leader Sheep

The Icelandic 'Leader Sheep'
are a distinct bloodline
within the herd. Both male
and female, they are seen as
dominant in their flocks

and have the ability
to run in front of the rest
when they are driven home
through heavy snowdrifts,
over ice covered ground,
or across rivers.

Sometimes the Leaders also
arrange taxis if the weather
is too harsh or a night
in the nearest Berghotel,
though believing their bodies

to be temples they insist
the mini bars are emptied
and the pay per view porn
channels are disconnected
in every sheep's room.

The Dark Ages

On the Moss of Cree
dank grass and scrub shoulder to the sea.
It's good for nothing land
that dissolves to a mosaic of mud,
and a few sheep scattered
like stoic punctuation marks.
How many pilgrims have
come ashore here in leather boats
on the way to Whithorn, to heaven,
and found driving rain and two men hacking
at a giant turnip with an axe?
Or someone playing a Gaelic lament on a banjo?
Or a traffic jam?
Yes unbelievably, we are in a traffic jam
inching our way to a Book Festival,
just another moment
in the bleak but oddly engaging history
of the Moss of Cree.

Sheep on a Snow Ridge

They are silent,
like witnesses to some sleight,
some ancient war
that only they remember.
At the crest of the hill
they stand in the snow
their presence a kind of memory
and also rebuke.
In all weathers the
questions they pose
are printed on the page of land.

The Ettrick Shepherd

Here you are in your great throne
with its rostrum of rams heads,
a seat set over sheep.
You look between the two lochs,
between two lives,
between the peasant and the celebrity,
between the Scots and the English,
between the lover and the puritan,
the sinner and saint,
between the moon and the ground:
like that poem you wrote
about the idiot boy screaming
at the sky not quite knowing
ever where it ended and the earth began.

Sheep Dog

Working dogs they say,
as if there was pay
and a car and a holiday
in Ibiza all inclusive.
Such lives they live.
Their tongues loll
and they are schooled to smile
like their old fathers,
below sad pools of eye.

James Hogg's Dog Blackie

When I first saw my dog Blackie he was being dragged by an ill natured drover, a scoundrel with a mark on his face like a footprint. As sour and surly a man I had never seen. But I took pity on the collie dog who looked ill kept but still gazed upon his master as though he was the lord of creation. I paid the owner, eliciting as I did the unwelcome news that the dog had suffered a childhood disease as a result of which he was 'hauf deif', and took the little fellow away with, given the circumstances of his early life, no great expectations of him mastering the skills expected of the noble border collie. I paid six shillings and never has money been so better spent, for Blackie, as I named him, turned out to be an avid learner and more than that so zealous in his desire to please his new master that his energy and enthusiasm was literally beyond computation.

Many are the tales of Blackie but I will recount one now in the expectation that it will act as a decent measurement of the dog's many admirable qualities.

Once in the most savage of winters I was delayed in literary matters in the town of Edinburgh, seeing the estimable Mr Blackwood, and came home to find that my entire flock of sheep some 300 strong had disappeared, being scared by the storm and had fetched up in a river valley swollen by flood and were in mortal danger of drowning in the night!

I poured myself a stiff measure of Old Combustible and prepared myself for bed fearing for the sight that would meet my eyes in the morning. 'Alack,' I said to Blackie, 'I fear tomorrow will see our ruin.' At this Blackie looked askance, as though he had not only heard every word but perfectly understood. After a few more strong measures, the better to fortify my spirits against the mordant thoughts that assailed me, I retired to bed and, at last, slept.

Imagine my surprise the next day when I swept back my curtains to find my herd restored in the Meadow, not a single creature harmed! It transpired that that most resourceful of creatures, Blackie, had heard my forebodings and acted to allay them, building rafts from fallen trees and, lashing them together with stout hemp rope, had rowed the whole herd to safe high ground! One group, stupidly resisting the dogs entreaties, were solicited to do so by Blackie patiently reading aloud from Mr Walter Scott's delightful 'Tales from the Inglenook' such a cheery vision of warmth being conjured up by the resourceful collie that the sheep could not help but meekly follow.

'Good, loyal dog,' I said, clapping him vigorously as you well might imagine, below his one good ear.

A second tale involving Blackie which has hitherto gone unheard has its origins in that wretched time when I was owner of Mitchellslacks, a small steading in Nithsdale. Those familiar with my tales *A Mountain Bard*, for the publication of which endless thanks are due to the estimable Messrs Constable and Cunningham, know well that my roots are in the country and with the common people and that I am a shepherd born of shepherds. I herded my first ewes in Ettrick at the age of seven, the same year I was bestowed by the muses with a love of the violin and of poetry. However a man who desires more in life than 'rough sack and rough sec' must needs plant coin and try and grow his fortune.

Unhappily my literary career, or so I idealised it, took up too much of my time as did frequent visits to my literary betters to try and secure what I perceived as 'the secrets' of success. As a result my commercial efforts failed and all too often I was at least 'half seas over', resorting to Old Combustible for succour.

In any case one evening I was ruminating on the inevitable foreclosure of my farm and the arrival of those appointed by the bailiff the next day to eject me and my rickle of belongings, nearly all worthless sentimental objects.

'Alack,' I said to Blackie, 'I fear tomorrow will see our ruin.' At this Blackie looked askance and then hard into the distance as though he knew exactly my meaning.

Those with some knowledge of the talents, zeal and resourcefulness of Blackie and the entire ancient tribe of the border collie may have some presentiment of what sight met my eyes the very next morning when I drew the curtains to let in the effusion of God's grace the sun, for there on the table was four hundred Guineas in brand new notes, signed and certified by the Clydesdale Bank of Commercial Street in the Port of Leith.

It transpired that Blackie had upon receiving my dire words the previous evening run the length of the Mennock Pass and over the Pentland Hills to rob the bank and then complete the return journey by dawn.

'Good, loyal dog,' I said, clapping him vigorously as you well might imagine, below both ears, including the deaf one.

Sheep Came Down at Christmas

On Christmas Eve sheep came down to Dalgarnock
because they had heard great events were to be discussed.
It was that rarest of things a parliament of sheep
and they had travelled down the hills from as far as Auchenlone,
Glenkens in the west, blackface and cheviot mostly,
though with other breeds mixed in.
The sheep talked through the evening, there was much to discuss.
They decided not to bomb Syria, noting that the Awassi sheep,
a breed active from Israel to Iraq, provided a model
of international cooperation.
They decided not to allow the security services
access to their personal information, and announced
a nuclear free zone from Thornhill to Clatteringshaws.
After that in spite of reiterating their atheism
the sheep sang quietly together for hours,
remembering that in the happiest moments
of religious iconography, from Mesopotamia to Palestine,
sheep have nearly always been present,
as the midwives of peace.

Sheep Poets Workshop Prompts

White lumps of firmament
Flock of cloud made solid
Straining against the five bar gates of life
We are the sheep who dream
Flying like confetti
Snow off the dyke
It's impermissible
Hiding in the fields
Apply for a bursary

Settlement

I spend a lot of time in the hills
but there are always sheep above me,
hanging in space on their stilt legs,
or at the very edge of my vision
circling crags like small clouds.

When the mountains crumble
into the new age of seas,
they will survive,
they will bump along the ocean floor
with blank expressions

chewing seaweed,
their lambs coming and going
quickly, like fish.
It will be a mystery how this will happen
but it will:

those with a bit of brain,
seeing the absurdity of their situation,
will drown, but the vast crowd,
having no doubts of their own,
will take it as read.

Cycle

The mountain   bone pit,
horn twists   table white
with knuckle   and skull   Where sky
begins

The dykes   spilled wool
cracks   splintered   banners
looped on wire   Where death
begins

Tree roots   shade
and safety   blood
streams of river   grass   Where life
begins

Old Tracks

Where do roads lead
now the tar is melting?
Surely into the same depths
of country,
across the same riverbeds.

Here in a rickle of stones
you can see the shape of a hearth,
a kitchen garden.
Did hollyhocks grow

against the wall here
patiently watered,
a blaze of colour thrown
on stone like paint?
Or bower vine?

Sheep know. The sun's scalpel
reveals the scratches
we make like cuneiform
on soil and rock

but always
the burnt grass parts
at each step they make,
the blades their crescent
path into the dead heart of a sun.

Sahil Island

When we first came
in our cedar ships
the carved horse head cutting the surf
we created a little part of the Levant
in this dough shaped place.

When they dig us up
in years to come may they
will feel our heat, our passion
born of the sun's full kiss,
wonder at our jumble of bones

in this casserole of soil,
our children with necklaces
of ivory
our cats, our hounds,
our sheep, all shared
our hearths.

The Golden Fleece

A neighbour told me once
that his father's best friend died
after a night in the Ram's Head
when he sat on the toilet
pulled the chain and the cistern
fell on his head.

Only now do I see
the heroic parallels with Jason
who having won the Golden Fleece
was resting while drunk
under the stern of the *Argo*
when it broke off and cracked his skull.

I suppose Auchinleck
is a bit like Iolcos
when the sun shines:
the years have
taken the lustre from lives
and only a glass glitters like gold.

The Path between the Mountains of the Moon

The joke is there is no path
between the Mountains of the Moon:
It is a local idiom. An impossibility,
like turning time.

Here we are, though, in a high wildness
of scrub and broken stone.
Only wild cabra have the nonchalance
to be here,

and buzzards riding thermals
above needle crags. When we pass
some bleached bones
I'm for going home

but my daughter says
'Don't you know
the best bits are always
just a little more uphill?'

and her long legs move
quickly, certainly, like the goats',
surging just ahead of me,
until she's lost in cloud.

Shooters

While men in ludicrous trousers
jostle to shoot flightless birds,
the sheep continue their
dialogue with grass.
They've seen them come
from far and wide
for slaughter
and overpriced Beaujolais.
Their florid faces wink
in the twilight like
ancient lanterns,
will o the wisps,
old gas escaping in one last rush.

The Old Fort at Grennan

Miles, and nothing alive
though an oystercatcher
calls somewhere, sadly.
Dykes twist to the horizon.
Where are the men who built them?
Gone to Nova Scotia
with their pipes and neckerchiefs.
On either side of the walls,
new wire restrains livestock
that's not there either,
to show that someone, somewhere,
owns this land, has a grant to prove it.
I climb, emerge onto the crest,
and a hare bounds off into cloud.
On top, with its boulders and sheep skulls,
its faint scars of ditch,
with a hollow wind through the thorns,
Grennan nails empty land to empty sky.

What Sheep Know

Leaves pasted,
little flames, on the door,
and the trees are done.
Summers wrecked in gardens,
upturned in blackening
beds of earth.
Hard by grey dykes
the sheep stand,
framed by haunches of cloud.
They've seen it all,
the Chardonnay and swingball,
the paddling pools
gone to mud and slugs.
What's forever in the hills?
A long chewing,
the fact a cold day will dawn.

Quhit Yowes Ken

Laevs klestirt
apo da door,
pierie lowes,
da tries kum døn.
Simmirs brukkit ati'jærds,
delld ati'mirknin
skittlins a'ært.
Tyght bie sjallmit dæks,
d'ir waatcht hit aa,
da Shardonnæ an swingba,
da paddlin pøls
kum guttir an slugs.
Quhit's etærnitil ati'da toons?
A laang showe,
da sooth o a kaald dæ's daan.

Translation by Robert Alan Jamieson

A Sheep and Duck Travel on the First Balloon Flight

Mais oui, d'accord,
le premier mouton,
le premier animal.
Regardez ci-dessous!

Je suis un pionnier, mon cher,
suspendu dans l'espace,
dans l'azure infinie,
dans le ciel de la poésie.

Et la rumeur que je n'étais pas le premier?
C'est un canard.

The Shades of One Shade

When I got up this morning
I saw the glint of a sea loch
in the cup's meniscus,
in the mirror behind my big head,
on the dank hillside like a mirage,
the sheep moving like buoys.
It's the stab of autumn.
Now sick summer's gone
with its smoke and mirrors
we can come into our own:
all the shades of one shade;
our stones, our seas,
our mountain tops,
our cold coming home.

Destiny

A sheep is trapped
under a five bar gate
on a slope near Balcary.
It is impossible to envisage how
this happened: there is no
fence or dyke
just a five bar gate
and a sheep trapped beneath,
and a mile of sky and waving grass
and the sea, endless and breaking.
I am alive and in love
and I lift the gate.
The sheep saunters off
to contemplate quietly
another strange suicide.

The View

The view down this hill
towards the violet and black water
of the Euchan this summer
evening is to pay for.
The hills are empty
but for sheep standing proprietorially
at empty doorways,
ruined kitchen gardens,
under roofs that leak stars.

Spring

(Pablo Picasso)

I am the curved blade
and backbone,
the sky shines through me,
pulses like a heart.
The earth is a green
sea broken on hills
and my crescent moons
are set now, hard in the sky.
Wake up!

The Adoration of the Shepherds

(Jusepi De Rivera)

Ye cin unerstaun ma hesitation people:
wasnae so much they toffs in thir
barbour jackets – I'm a cheviot
an used to yon malarkey –
it wasnae Jesus eether
nice wee chap,
scrubs up weel, ye hae tae say,
it wasnae even whit wis goin oan
on the ceiling,
a these weans wi curls and wings –
ca me mental but
ahve no bin able tae skek at weans oan
a ceiling since Trainspottin –
whit had me reely sweatin
was a yon goggle-eened rapture
in the bothy.
Ony time there's joy in the Bible,
a sheep gets it.

The Sound of Sheep Is Like the Sound of Poetry

Beyond the filigree of bird song,
the fret-work so to say,

sheep speak morning and night
and won't be quietened.

When you tune your ears in,
it is monotonous and terrifying.

They are like the two tribes
of poetry. Bah! one shouts, Bad!

and the other, trying hard
to catch the eye of a guest writer

or minor literary celebrity
shouts Me! Me! Me!

Fighting Sheep

'Kbabshis, coaches of Algerian fighting sheep are tough but also surprisingly tender. They treat their sheep like mistresses, stopping by the garages where they install them, bringing food, caressing and massaging them before they head out together for long walks on the beach.'

Thunder tonight
the sea is electric with tears
the affesas dips its head

I who have nothing
have less than nothing now:
Yasmine is dead

her skull cracked
like baked clay
under a red sickle moon.

The Trouble with Science

'Dolly is derived from a mammary gland cell
and we couldn't think of a more impressive pair
of glands than Dolly Parton's'.
Sad sexists don't have to be cloned,
there are a million of them.
Some of them are even geniuses
but matters of life and death and playing God
you might imagine would be undertaken
by someone with sensitivity and taste
maybe even a love of literature.
The Pyrenean Ibex brought briefly
back after the long extinction of its race
lived a few short breaths.
Not enough to be named after
some tits but long enough
you would think
for a poem.

The Inadequacy of Sheep Metaphors

'They followed like sheep'
seems to me a stupid simile.
I look at sheep and they run like fuck
when you come near,
wriggle through impossible gaps.
Wag shitty tails at you
as they disappear.
They seem a feisty lot
and largely, while they're alive,
please themselves.
We make similes like that
while we're on our way to work
or collecting weans from drama
or examining bank statements
or mowing the lawn
or shrugging our shoulders at injustice
or not living for love
or measuring the years drop
from shelves like wholly unread books.

Castle Sheep

Mist on water,
reeds like drowning arms.
We move on this landscape
and always loch and light shivers.
It would be easy to be lost here:
we fall in and out of dreams,
and could die as easily as lose our way.
Night takes everything
and soon there is just our noise, then less,
breath, stars are sewn in gold at last,
and cold's a kiss.

Simple Truths

Behind the births of nations
the symbols and the exposition,
the simple sacred words of our people.
Waltzing Matilda, Lochaber No More,
the dead swagman and his jumbuck,
the dog and the weeping shepherd.

Wire

Framed in wire
this world of wet earth
and grass: we see
it all in easy chunks of maths.

The wire divides us:
the patchwork that keeps
real life at bay,
a no man's land combed

by tractor and subsidy
and slurry. A featureless paste
below sullen skies.
Trees bend at the edges:

they are on the front line
and know it.
The wire defines us.
Who dares stop simple progress?

in the evening the miles of wire
burn like blood,
threads of fleece
streaming like lost flags.

After the Sheep

Never has a field been so empty.
Though it is bright as the sea
and moves with a fresh wind
down the glen,
it is the green of desolation.
The paths wandering its edge,

the tracks of the quad bike
disappearing like archaeology,
are like half finished sentences,
letters hurriedly written
before deportation and death.
We will forget.

Come Live with Me

We shall describe
the movement of water,
why trees glow thick as paint.
Our words will be living,
like children. They will grow
into books and the books
into volumes of books.
Like sheep they will fill the world
and we will tend them
from our hut,
from our tree house,
from our cranny in the clouds.
As long as we live
the flocks and herds of words
will wander wearing our hearts.

December in Penpont

Sheep have returned to the glebe,
their breath rises solid in the air.
The wing of earth bare
to the bones of the silent church,

a slow and careful choir now,
of movement and ritual.
No talk for another while
of overflow car parks

just an ancient meeting
in the eye of beasts and land,
the parched winter sky and then,
if we're lucky again, stars.

Sheep Ends

If you're a sheep
it must be a great struggle
to escape symbolism.
It's much worse than goat pox
scrapie or blue tongue
or the blizzards that sweep
border hills or the nip and bark of dogs
or even the pain of separation.
What a burden to be the most
common noun in the bible
after Lord, God and Israel
and yet not have a single speaking part?
It's bad enough being used
for food but metaphor is worse.
One day a great Sheep lawyer
and liberator will corner God
and hold him to his word at last.
'You said you would "place the sheep
at your right hand and the goats at your left".
Here we are.'

The Bird on the Sheep's Back

The bird on the sheep's back
has foregone altitude:
a sheep is a different kind
of cloud moving certainly, but rooted.

Perhaps it tires of the sweep
and the thermals, of the blinding blue,
the unimaginable tracts of colour,
maybe it thinks it's better

at ground level
with the old sheep
going forever clockwise,
moving in small steps
but further.

Circles

The sheep move mysteriously
clockwise, field to field.
I see them on my own little trails.
We have our eyes
cast down the sheep and I,
at our feet.
When occasionally
our gazes meet
it is a rueful exchange:
Are we thinking how
unlucky the other is to be
slouched in a sodden coat
this October morning
circling a watery sun?
Or are we thinking that
circles will be broken,
nothing surer.

King of the Sheep

Ramhorn xxv out of Clon Dubh
surveys his concubines
and pronounces his balls
the most swollen in Western Europe.
Even old men in trilbies
and faded waxed jackets
sweat and salivate
as he preens and struts
his stuff. He is sexual.
The auctioneer trembles
on the edge of economic orgasm.

Luath Press Limited

committed to publishing well written books worth reading

LUATH PRESS takes its name from Robert Burns, whose little collie Luath (*Gael.*, swift or nimble) tripped up Jean Armour at a wedding and gave him the chance to speak to the woman who was to be his wife and the abiding love of his life. Burns called one of the 'Twa Dogs' Luath after Cuchullin's hunting dog in Ossian's *Fingal*. Luath Press was established in 1981 in the heart of Burns country, and is now based a few steps up the road from Burns' first lodgings on Edinburgh's Royal Mile. Luath offers you distinctive writing with a hint of unexpected pleasures.

Most bookshops in the UK, the US, Canada, Australia, New Zealand and parts of Europe, either carry our books in stock or can order them for you. To order direct from us, please send a £sterling cheque, postal order, international money order or your credit card details (number, address of cardholder and expiry date) to us at the address below. Please add post and packing as follows: UK – £1.00 per delivery address; overseas surface mail – £2.50 per delivery address; overseas airmail – £3.50 for the first book to each delivery address, plus £1.00 for each additional book by airmail to the same address. If your order is a gift, we will happily enclose your card or message at no extra charge.

Luath Press Limited
543/2 Castlehill
The Royal Mile
Edinburgh EH1 2ND
Scotland
Telephone: +44 (0)131 225 4326 (24 hours)
Email: sales@luath. co.uk
Website: www. luath.co.uk